EVERGLADES
National Park

by Ruth Radlauer

Design and photographs
by Rolf Zillmer

AN ELK GROVE BOOK

 CHILDRENS PRESS, CHICAGO

Bequest of Beauty

A bequest is a gift for those who
follow. Each National Park is a
BEQUEST OF BEAUTY. It is a place of
special interest or beauty that has
been saved by the United States government
especially for you, your children, and
their great-great-grandchildren. This
bequest is yours to have and to care for
so that others who follow can do the same
during their lives.

With thanks to the men and women
who add enjoyment to the National Parks,
the Park Rangers, and especially to
Mr. Pat Crosland, Assistant Chief Naturalist,
Everglades National Park.

Library of Congress Cataloging in Publication Data
Radlauer, Ruth Shaw.
  Everglades National Park.
  (National Parks, bequest of beauty series)
  ''An Elk Grove book.''
  SUMMARY: Describes some of the plants and animals
of the Everglades National Park and suggests ways to
enjoy this unique Park to the fullest.
    1. Everglades National Park—Juvenile literature.
[1. Everglades National Park]   I. Zillmer, Rolf.
II. Title.   III. Series.
F317.E9R3   917.59'39   75-11773
ISBN 0-516-07488-1

Copyright © 1975 by Regensteiner Publishing Enterprises, Inc.
All rights reserved. Published simultaneously in Canada.
Printed in the United States of America

6 7 8 9 10 11 12 13 14 15 R 81

Contents

What is Everglades National Park?

Everglades National Park is a huge flat place covered with sawgrass growing in water. Here and there a raised island called a hammock dots the "river of grass," and a mangrove forest grows around the bay and gulf edges of the park.

Everglades is the sight of alligators sleeping in the sun or the sight of birds flocking to Mrazek Pond.

It's the itch of a mosquito bite or it may be the feel of the snake you hold when a Park Ranger tells you it won't bite.

Everglades is an early morning birdwatch or a walk in the swamp with a Ranger. It's a canoe trip through channels of the mangrove forest or a hike on the Pineland Trail.

This park is the smell of a million green plants growing in rich, wet peat and the salty smell of a sea breeze. It's the sound of ducks landing on the water and the scolding squawk of a little green heron.

It's Florida's wet land, one of the wettest United States National Parks.

Pinelands In The Everglades

Shark Valley Alligators

Mrazek Pond

Water Snake

Canoeing

Where is Everglades National Park?

Everglades National Park is a small part of the Florida Everglades. You can get there from Miami or another Florida town called Naples.

The best way to see the park may be on a bicycle, but most people go through the park by car. Plan to stay at each stop in the park for an hour or two. Take time to soak up all the wonder.

At Royal Palm there are two wonders: the Anhinga Trail and Gumbo Limbo Trail. The Anhinga Trail's wonders are animals such as alligators, turtles, and birds. Plant wonders await you in the green jungle of the Gumbo Limbo Trail.

On the drive south to Flamingo are the Pineland Trail and ponds where you can see the big birds. Raised boardwalk trails go through tree islands called hammocks.

From the west entrance to the park, you can go first to Gulf Coast. Here boat cruises and canoe trips take you to the Ten Thousand Islands.

And don't miss Shark Valley with its tower where you may see wood storks and alligators by the dozen.

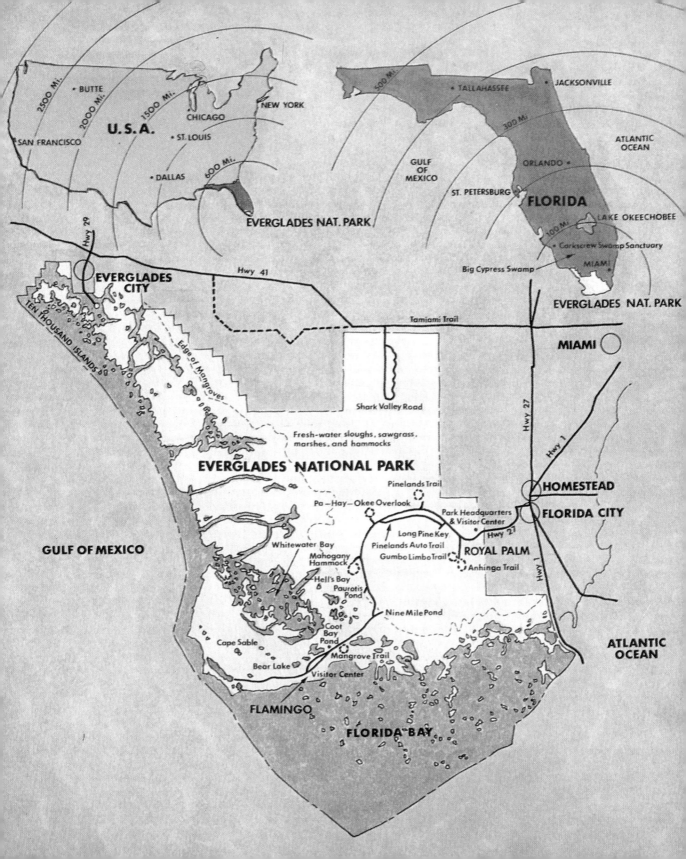

A Walk in the Swamp

The best way to know and feel the Everglades is to go for a walk in the swamp with a Park Ranger. For this walk, called a slough (sloo) slog or swamp tromp, you need old long pants and tennis shoes.

At Paurotis Pond the swamp tromp starts out in the water and goes to a hammock which is an island of trees. The sound of people scares some of the wildlife away, but you may see lizards, birds, snails, and crabs. And you see how the red mangrove builds the land.

On another swamp tromp you walk across squishy gray periphyton. In the wet summer, many tiny water plants called algae grow together to make periphyton. In the dry winter, periphyton holds water and allows fish eggs and tiny water life to stay alive.

Soon the tromp comes to a cypress head, or grove, which the Ranger says has grown out of a "gator hole."

"What," you ask, "is a gator hole?"

page 8

Gator Holes

A gator hole is made by the park's famous reptile, the alligator. This reptile seems to know that summer rain will stop, and dry winter will follow.

To hold water that it must have to live, an alligator digs a hole. Fish, insects, and plants grow in and around the hole. Year after year the alligator digs and makes the hole wider and wider. Trees grow around the pond and this becomes what is called a cypress head.

Many kinds of plants grow in the cypress head. Wild pickerel weed brings deer to browse among its blue flowers. Air plants cling to the trees where they live off debris and dust from the air rather than soil. One air plant called the wild pine holds water in its cup-like leaves, and lizards drink from them.

A gator hole helps plants and animals live through the dry season and may become the center of a cypress head. Sometimes the mound made by the alligator's digging is the beginning for a hammock.

These are some of the reasons why alligators are so important to the Everglades.

Cypress In A Gator Hole

Wild Pickerel Weed

Air Plant

Alligators

You may see a gator hole on a swamp tromp, but the best places to see alligators are at Shark Valley or on the Anhinga Trail.

A mother alligator leaves the gator hole to build her nest in the sawgrass. In late May or early June she lays 30 to 60 eggs and covers them with sticks, grass, and leaves. She guards the nest while she goes back and forth between the gator hole and sawgrass.

Nine weeks later, the babies peck at their eggs and call, "Rrmp, rrmp." The mother hears and digs them out of the nest. Of the 30 to 60 eggs, only 10 or 20 hatch. The baby alligators are between 6 and 12 inches long. Their mother doesn't feed them, but she protects them for as long as two years while they eat fish and grow about a foot a year. Alligators also eat turtles, birds, and any other animals that get too close.

Sometimes a mother may have new babies and year-old ones with her at the same time. This is a time when any animal is most dangerous, when it's protecting its young.

gator

Alligator

by Alligators

Alligator

Snakes

Among other reptiles in the Everglades are 24 kinds of snakes. Only 4 are poisonous: the diamondback and pygmy rattlesnakes, the coral snake, and the water mocassin, or cottonmouth.

All snakes are afraid of people, so if you watch carefully, you can stay away from poisonous ones. A snake's color often matches the plants around it. That's why you have to look carefully to see a cottonmouth by a wilderness trail.

Park Rangers capture non-poisonous snakes and keep them in cages for a while and you can see them in a daily program at Flamingo Visitor Center. Most of the snakes are very gentle, so you can hold them if you are gentle, too.

Probably the biggest and gentlest is the indigo snake. Many people have made pets out of indigo snakes. For that reason, and because their living space is being used up by towns and farms, the indigo snake is getting rare.

The speckled Florida king snake lives on the ground and eats other snakes, even poisonous ones except for the coral snake.

onmouth Or Water Mocassin

Indigo Snake

ida King Snake

Other Reptiles

Other reptiles in the Everglades are turtles, lizards, and crocodiles. Reptiles are cold-blooded animals. Their blood is as warm or cold as the air or water around them. When they're cold, they are not active. When they are warm, they move around, hunt, eat, mate, and lay eggs.

Crocodiles live near salt water, but alligators need fresh water. Crocodiles are olive green, while their cousins are almost black. A crocodile's snout is pointed compared with the alligator's, but you won't get much chance to compare these two reptiles because crocodiles are so shy. They're also getting rare.

You may not see a crocodile, but you might see a little green lizard called the anole or false chameleon. The anole can change color from bright green to brown or gray. The false chameleon changes color because of things like air temperature or fear. A flap of loose skin on the male's throat forms a bright red fan when it tries to scare away another male or to attract a female.

Anole Or False Chameleon ►

The Mangrove Forest

The red mangrove tree is called a land builder because its roots trap debris such as sticks, grass, and leaves. This debris decays and becomes soil. The mangrove holds the soil and keeps it from washing away in the high winds and rain of a hurricane.

Other trees drop seeds that grow into new trees. Because the salty soil under mangroves is not good for sprouting seeds, the mangrove holds its seeds until they start to grow into plants, or seedlings.

In late August these live seedlings drop into the water. Some seedlings may take root under the tree. Others float as far as a thousand miles away. When it reaches shallow water or a sandbar, the seedling takes root and begins to grow.

A year later the seedling sends out prop roots that take food and water from the soil. The prop roots make the tree strong enough to stand against hurricanes.

Many kinds of animals live in the mangrove forest. Tree oysters cling to the prop roots. Panthers and bobcats hunt raccoons and marsh rabbits, and snakes, lizards, and birds make their homes in the mangrove forest.

Mangrove Forest, A Land Builder

Red Mangrove Seedling

Red Mangrove Prop Roots

Red Mangrove

Apple Snails

When you walk across the swamp in the dry season, you may see many dead shells that look like Ping-Pong balls. Alive, these were shiny brown apple snails. Many animals eat them, but a rare bird called the Everglades kite eats nothing but apple snails.

An apple snail feeds under water on tiny plants and animals. It has a lung, so it must come up out of the water to breathe. Then the Everglades kite swoops down and grabs it with one foot. But now the supply of apple snails is getting so small that there are less than 100 kites left.

The apple snail lays its eggs on the grass above the water. If the glades get too dry, the snails can't live. If the glades are too wet, the eggs may be eaten by fish or rot in the water. Sometimes a fire kills the snails. Their biggest enemy may be humans whose farms, canals, and cities upset the dry-wet cycle.

At a wildlife refuge near the park people are growing apple snails to save the Everglades kite from extinction.

Apple Snail

Apple Snail Eggs

Tree Snails — Liguus

Another rare snail is the tree snail called Liguus, or lig. A Liguus can have one of over 50 different color combinations. Ligs cling like jewels to the smooth bark of hardwood trees that grow in hammocks. During the wet season they eat lichen, which is a combination of two tiny plants, fungus and alga.

During the dry season these "jewels" seal themselves to smooth bark in a protected place. Here they "sleep" or estivate for months until the rains return. A Liguus can even estivate while the limb to which it is sealed is blown miles away by a hurricane.

Outside the park, builders destroy hammocks, and ligs are vanishing. Inside Everglades National Park, Rangers are trying to save the tree snail by "planting" some in hammocks of the park.

Tree Snail Or Liguus ►

Golden Orb Spider

If you look carefully along any trail, you'll find the beautiful webs of golden orb spiders. The golden orb spins a giant web about a metre or yard wide.

The silk strands of the web are stronger than those of the silk worm. Some people used to twist these strands together and make fish nets. Others weave beautiful fabrics from them.

Since some of the strands are very sticky, the spider has to be careful not to get caught in its own web. The sticky strands of the web catch beetles and flies for the spider's food.

The female golden orb also eats her smaller mate and sometimes another large female. The young spiders eat each other as soon as they hatch.

You might think the golden orb's strange eating habits would cause it to die off. Instead, this habit means that only the strongest spiders live to have young.

Birds

You may not be a birdwatcher when you come to Everglades National Park. But if you stay even one day, you will become a birdwatcher. You can't help it.

About 300 kinds of birds have been seen in the park. Some live there all year, while others are only winter or summer visitors. The park has marsh birds, waders, and waterfowl, as well as land birds.

One marsh bird, the white ibis, is easy to recognize. Its long beak curves down, and its wings are tipped with black.

The little green heron is a wader that uses a tool. If it sees no fish in the water, it will drop a leaf or twig to attract a fish, then catch it. This squawky little bird's headfeathers ruffle up when it gets excited.

Many kinds of herons live in the park. They are the little blue, the great blue, great white, and Louisiana herons. Two kinds of bitterns, which are also herons, and two kinds of night herons are harder to find.

With binoculars or a telescope you will find more birds to enjoy watching.

White Ibis And Little Green Heron

Birdwatching

The best times to see birds are the early morning and late afternoon during the dry season from December to April.

Many people go out early and watch before the sun comes up. Sometimes a Ranger sets up a telescope and you can get a look at some of the birds of prey called raptors. At Coot Bay Pond you can look through the telescope at a raptor's nest. Two bald eagles have been nesting for several years about a mile from there.

Another raptor, the osprey, builds a big nest in the mangrove trees.

Binoculars or a telescope can help you find a great blue heron catching a fish. At the same pond you may see the great egret taking flight.

Over Florida Bay you will see pelicans, frigate birds, and black skimmers. A black skimmer flies over the water until it sees a fish. Then it swoops and skims a fish out of the water with its lower beak which is longer than the upper beak.

Osprey

Great Blue Heron

Great Egret

Skimmers

Strange Beaks

Brown pelicans nest on the mangrove islands called keys in Florida Bay. You can see them from Flamingo as they fly low over the water, dive, and catch fish in the pouches under their beaks.

The white pelican, a visitor from the north, wades in shallow water and nets its fish with its pouch.

Many people expect to see flamingos in the park, but only a few of them come to the mud flats where not many visitors go. Their true home is in the Bahama Islands east of Florida.

Between November and March you may see roseate spoonbills around mangrove keys and sometimes at Bear Lake.

A young spoonbill takes three years to get all of its rosy feathers. This bird wades on its long red legs in shallow water and swings its spoon-like beak from side to side. The "spoon" of the spoonbill's beak is a big grabber, so it grabs lots of fish.

Years of protection in the park have saved the spoonbill which was almost extinct in the 1940s.

Roseate Spoonbill ►

Wood Storks

The wood stork is a big bird that lives on fish. It may soon vanish because when the wet-dry cycle is upset, the wood stork will not mate, or breed.

After a good wet season, there are many fish. As the weather turns dry, the fish crowd into ponds. This crowding of fish gives the wood stork enough to eat during the breeding season. During the 4 months of nesting and caring for the young, a wood stork family with two babies needs 440 pounds of fish.

The wood stork never returns to its nest with an empty beak. It carries a fish to feed the young or a stick to add to the nest. Because its bones are very light, the wood stork must be careful to balance things in its beak. That's why it throws a stick up and catches it a few times until the stick is balanced. Then the stork takes off in flight.

In the park, Shark Valley is a good place to look for wood storks. They are also protected outside the park at the Corkscrew Sanctuary.

Wood Storks

Wood Stork Ready To Fly

Nesting Wood Storks

Biking and Hiking

Flat! That's what the Everglades National Park is. Most of the park is only 2 or 3 feet above sea level. That's why it's such a good place to ride a bicycle.

Biking along the road through the quiet sawgrass prairie, you look out at blue sky and fluffy white clouds. It's easy pedaling, and it feels good to see so far into the distance.

If you want to see wildlife, hiking may be better than biking since the noise and movement of a bike can scare the animals away. The Flamingo area has several day hikes that are 2 to 7 miles long. Ask a Ranger for the map that includes Coastal Prairie, Bear Lake, Snake Bight, and other trails.

On the long hike to Alligator Creek, you'll find a campground where you can stay. Besides camping equipment, you'll need insect repellent and water. As in canoe camping, you must bring out of the backcountry everything that you take in. You also need a permit to go into the backcountry and a fishing license to fish in fresh water.

Ranger-guided Bike Trip ►

Trails — Anhinga and Gumbo Limbo

In the Royal Palm area of the park are two trails you must not miss, the Anhinga and Gumbo Limbo Trails.

On the Anhinga Trail you are sure to see the anhinga, a bird that is also called the snakebird because of its snake-like neck. The anhinga swims under water until it finds a fish and spears it with its sharp beak. Then it climbs to a branch and spreads its wings to dry. It probably wants to get warm as well as dry. Wouldn't you?

You'll also see alligators, turtles, garfish, bream, and bass, as well as herons and egrets on Anhinga Trail.

The Gumbo Limbo Trail is named for the gumbo limbo tree. The lightweight wood of this tree has been carved into merry-go-round horses. A hurricane cannot destroy this tree. If it gets blown over, any part of it that touches the ground sends out roots and goes on growing. The Gumbo Limbo Trail is like a jungle with about 70 kinds of plants and many small animals, so keep your eyes open!

Anhinga Trail

Anhinga Bird

Bark Of The Gumbo Limbo Tree

Other Nature Trails

Many more trails await you, some short enough for even the laziest walker. Along the trails, labels near some of the plants explain how they grow and why they are important.

The park is dryer where the ground is high, and 4 to 6 feet above sea level is high in the Everglades! Pines grow on this higher, dryer ground. On the Pineland Trail you will see South Florida slash pine along with the coontie and saw-palmetto. These plants do well after fires because fire keeps out the shady, hardwood trees that would crowd them out.

Hardwood trees like mahogany and oak grow in hammocks. A raised boardwalk trail takes you through the Mahogany Hammock where you will see the biggest mahogany tree in the country. You'll see the strangler fig, too. This tree attaches itself to another host tree. Then the strangler fig begins to grow on the host's branch or trunk. It sends roots down to the ground. Winding itself around the host, it gets so big that it chokes or strangles the host.

Pinelands

Strangler Fig

Camping and Fishing

Both you and the birds will find fishing in the Everglades National Park pretty good. In the dry season, the fish gather in the ponds as the water drains out of the sawgrass. A person can also fish from the beach at Flamingo or from a rented canoe or boat.

You must have a fishing license for fresh water fishing, but no license is needed for salt water fishing unless you plan to sell what you catch. There are limits according to size, and you may only take a certain number at a time. Other rules are against collecting and feeding fish, and some kinds like starfish and seahorses are protected.

You can camp with tents, trailers, or campers at Long Pine Key and Flamingo. Both of these campgrounds have water, and Flamingo has showers.

If you hike in the backcountry or go on long canoe trips, you can camp at many campsites. Remember that you must carry out *everything* you take into the backcountry.

Canoeing

Everglades National Park is a good place to paddle a canoe. You can take day-long trips with a Ranger or go with a friend, but never alone. If canoeing is new to you, the Ranger will show you how to paddle.

A canoe trip starts when you write your float plan at the beginning of the canoe trail. The float plan tells where you plan to go and when you should be back.

You won't get lost if you follow the numbered white stakes that mark all trails. The easiest canoeing goes over the 12-mile Bear Lake Trail where you can see lots of wildlife and go fishing. Another easy, 7-hour trip is from West Lake to a campground at Alligator Creek.

The hardest trails are Noble Hammock, Hell's Bay, and Wilderness Waterway. It takes 7 days to go 100 miles by canoe on the Wilderness Waterway from Everglades City to Flamingo. Most of the 10 camps along the way have tables and other things you need for camping.

Canoeing At Bear Lake ►

Wildlife

If you go canoeing or camping, you will see more wildlife than other Everglades visitors do. Many different animals live here, but many of them are rare. Crocodiles, Everglades kites, and two sea mammals, the manatee and bottlenose dolphin, are about to vanish.

With luck you will see bobcats and raccoons in the mangrove wilderness. In fresh water sloughs near Shark Valley, you may find a playful otter crunching on an apple snail.

One of the rarest sights is a panther, also known as a cougar, puma, painter, catamount, or mountain lion. Panthers live in some of the hardwood hammocks and in the mangrove forest.

The panther preys on deer and small mammals. Because the panther has been hunted and almost killed off, raccoons are getting more plentiful.

Many animals hunt mostly at night and hide or sleep during the day, so you'll see more of them in the early morning or evening.

Panther ►

Everglades or Neverglades?

Many national parks are high in the mountains where the water supply comes from rain and melting snow. Those parks have use of the water first before it flows on down to farms and cities.

Everglades water comes from rain and from Lake Okeechobee and Big Cypress Swamp. Years ago people wanted to build cities and farms, so they tried to drain the swamp. Roads and canals were built across the glades. Now people often use up water that should go to the Everglades. At other times flood control lets water enter the glades when they should be drying out. The "forever glades" are in danger of being the "never glades."

The summer-wet, winter-dry cycle has been changed by man, and the wildlife is in danger. The wilderness and animals such as the wood stork will vanish unless the Everglades water supply is protected.

It's hard to know what is most important. We need food from farms. We need houses to live in. But we also need a wilderness where people can go for a quiet visit with nature.

What is your answer, Everglades or Neverglades?

About the Author and Illustrator

Ruth Radlauer's love affair with nature and National Parks began in Wyoming where she spent her summers at camp in Casper Mountain or traveling with her family in Yellowstone National Park.

Mr. and Mrs. Radlauer, graduates of University of California at Los Angeles, are authors of many books for young people age three to thirteen. Their subjects range from social studies to youth activities such as horse riding and motorcycles.

Photographing the National Parks is a labor of love for Rolf Zillmer and his wife Evelyn. The Zillmers get an intimate view of each park since they are backpack and wildlife enthusiasts.

A former student at Art Center College of Design in Los Angeles, Mr. Zillmer was born in New York City and now makes his home in California where he is the Art Director for Elk Grove Books.

Photo Credits: Cover, Alligator, Baby Alligators p. 13,

Indigo Snake p. 15, Apple Snail p. 21 by Ed Radlauer.